WORKBOOK 1

prepared for the course team by norma sherratt,
david goldblatt, maureen mackintosh and kath woodward

This publication forms part of an Open University course DD100 *An Introduction to the Social Sciences: Understanding Social Change*. Details of this and other Open University courses can be obtained from the Course Information and Advice Centre, PO Box 724, The Open University, Milton Keynes MK7 6ZS, United Kingdom: tel. +44 (0)1908 653231, e-mail general-enquiries@open.ac.uk

Alternatively, you may visit the Open University website at http://www.open.ac.uk where you can learn more about the wide range of courses and packs offered at all levels by The Open University.

To purchase a selection of Open University course materials visit the webshop at www.ouw.co.uk, or contact Open University Worldwide, Michael Young Building, Walton Hall, Milton Keynes MK7 6AA, United Kingdom for a brochure. tel. +44 (0)1908 858785; fax +44 (0)1908 858787; e-mail ouwenq@open.ac.uk

The Open University
Walton Hall, Milton Keynes
MK7 6AA

First published 2000. Second edition 2001. Third edition 2004

Edited, designed and typeset by The Open University.

Printed and bound in the United Kingdom by the Alden Group, Oxford

ISBN 0 7492 5362 2

3.1

31057B/dd100wb1i3.1

Contents

The DD100 course team

John Allen, *Professor of Geography*

Penny Bennett, *Editor*

Pam Berry, *Compositor*

Simon Bromley, *Senior Lecturer in Government*

Lydia Chant, *Course Manager*

Stephen Clift, *Editor*

Allan Cochrane, *Professor of Public Policy*

Lene Connolly, *Print Buying Controller*

Jonathan Davies, *Graphic Designer*

Graham Dawson, *Lecturer in Economics*

Ross Fergusson, *Staff Tutor in Social Policy (Region 02)*

Fran Ford, *Senior Course Co-ordination Secretary*

Ian Fribbance, *Staff Tutor in Economics (Region 01)*

David Goldblatt, *Co-Course Team Chair*

Richard Golden, *Production and Presentation Administrator*

Jenny Gove, *Lecturer in Psychology*

Peter Hamilton, *Lecturer in Sociology*

Celia Hart, *Picture Researcher*

David Held, *Professor of Politics and Sociology*

Susan Himmelweit, *Professor of Economics*

Stephen Hinchliffe, *Lecturer in Geography*

Wendy Hollway, *Professor of Psychology*

Gordon Hughes, *Senior Lecturer in Social Policy*

Wendy Humphreys, *Staff Tutor in Government (Region 01)*

Jonathan Hunt, *Co-publishing Advisor*

Christina Janoszka, *Course Manager*

Pat Jess, *Staff Tutor in Geography (Region 12)*

Bob Kelly, *Staff Tutor in Government (Region 06)*

Margaret Kiloh, *Staff Tutor in Social Policy (Region 13)*

Sylvia Lay-Flurrie, *Secretary*

Gail Lewis, *Senior Lecturer in Social Policy*

Siân Lewis, *Graphic Designer*

Liz McFall, *Lecturer in Sociology*

Tony McGrew, *Professor of International Relations, University of Southampton*

Hugh Mackay, *Staff Tutor in Sociology (Region 10)*

Maureen Mackintosh, *Professor of Economics*

Eugene McLaughlin, *Senior Lecturer in Criminology and Social Policy*

Andrew Metcalf, *Senior Producer, BBC*

Gerry Mooney, *Staff Tutor in Social Policy (Region 11)*

Lesley Moore, *Senior Course Co-ordination Secretary*

Ray Munns, *Graphic Artist*

Karim Murji, *Senior Lecturer in Sociology*

Sarah Neal, *Lecturer in Social Policy*

Kathy Pain, *Staff Tutor in Geography (Region 02)*

Clive Pearson, *Tutor Panel*

Ann Phoenix, *Professor of Psychology*

Lynn Poole, *Tutor Panel*

Raia Prokhovnik, *Senior Lecturer in Government*

Norma Sherratt, *Staff Tutor in Sociology (Region 03)*

Roberto Simonetti, *Lecturer in Economics*

Dick Skellington, *Project Officer*

Brenda Smith, *Staff Tutor in Psychology (Region 12)*

Mark Smith, *Senior Lecturer in Government*

Matt Staples, *Course Manager*

Grahame Thompson, *Professor of Political Economy*

Ken Thompson, *Professor of Sociology*

Diane Watson, *Staff Tutor in Sociology (Region 05)*

Stuart Watt, *Lecturer in Psychology*

Andy Whitehead, *Graphic Artist*

Kath Woodward, *Course Team Chair, Senior Lecturer in Sociology*

Chris Wooldridge, *Editor*

External Assessor

Nigel Thrift, *Professor of Geography, University of Bristol*

INTRODUCTION

You will be working on Block 1 of the course for the next five weeks, with this workbook as your guide and with a whole week set aside for writing TMA 01 at the end. In a moment you will be starting on the Introduction and Chapter 1 of the book *Questioning Identity: Gender, Class, Ethnicity*. Before this we want to spend a little time preparing you for Block 1.

Block overview

As with all your work on DD100, Block 1 includes a range of teaching materials, including: the textbook *Questioning Identity*, this workbook, audio-cassettes, and a TV programme (see Figure 1 below). As with the Introductory Block, you will need to think about how to organize your time and what route to take through the materials. The recommended route is shown in Figure 2. Please check the *Study Calendar* for TV programme broadcast times – we recognize that TV schedules and your working patterns may not coincide.

Study week	Course material	Suggested study time
4	*Workbook 1* and Book 1: *Questioning Identity: Gender, Class, Ethnicity* Introduction Chapter 1 Audio-cassette 3, Side A	1 hour $10\frac{1}{2}$ hours 30 minutes
5	Workbook and Chapter 2	12 hours
6	Workbook and Chapter 3 *Study Skills Supplement 1: Reading Visual Images,* plus Audio-cassette 2	10 hours 2 hours
7	Workbook and Chapter 4 Afterword TV 01: *Defining Moments* Audio-cassette 3, Side B	$9\frac{1}{2}$ hours 1 hour 1 hour 30 minutes
8	TMA 01	12 hours

FIGURE 1   Course materials for Block 1

FIGURE 2   Recommended study route for Block I

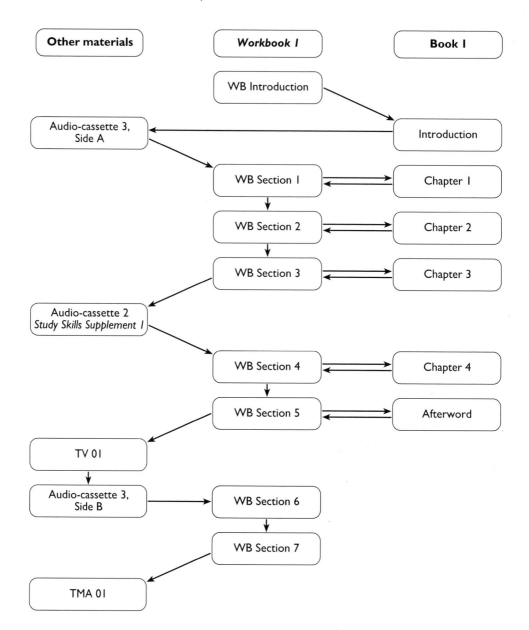

Key questions

DD100 is question driven and Block 1 is no exception. It is worth just stopping for a moment to think about the three key framing questions of the block.

I   How are identities formed?

Identities are a complex matter. They are our way of describing who we think we are, as individuals and as part of wider social groups. How do we acquire our identities? By what processes do we come to know who we are? To what extent are our identities formed in our childhood? Do they continue to develop and change? Once established are identities fixed or do we have to constantly re-create our identities?

2   To what extent can we shape our own identities?

As you might have recognized, thinking about the formation of identity draws on the course theme of *structure and agency*. How far is what happens to us, as individuals and social groups, a result of our own wishes, intentions and decisions? To what extent are there other forces at work which are beyond our control? What might these forces be?

3   Are there uncertainties about identity in the UK?

If by identity we mean who we think we are and how others see us, then it does seem that for many people identities may not be as certain as they were in the past. All kinds of economic, social and cultural changes appear to have generated more uncertainty about who we are. The role models and experiences of earlier generations may be less reliable guides to identity today. We may have a number of different, possibly conflicting, identities presenting us with problems earlier generations never had to face.

Key skills

Alongside these framing questions of identity, your work on Block 1 will develop a key range of social science skills and study skills. These include:

- understanding the production of social science knowledge, through what we have called the *circuit of knowledge*;

- understanding how a social science argument is constructed, and the role of concepts and theories in its construction;

- learning to work with quantitative and qualitative evidence;

- learning to read visual images, including maps;

- developing some writing skills and techniques;

- developing your skills as an independent learner – in particular some techniques for using your tutor, the telephone and self-help groups to the best advantage.

In addition, as part of your work on Block 1, we will be helping you to develop the active reading and note-taking skills you began working on in the Introductory Block. Most of these skills are developed in Sections 1–4 of this workbook, in combination with your study of other course materials. Section 5 gives you an opportunity to consolidate and reflect on your work, while Section 6 picks up the independent learner skills. In Section 7 of this workbook we will turn to questions of assessment.

Assessing Block I

At the end of your work on this block you will have an assignment (TMA 01) to send to your tutor. The questions set for the assignment will be different each year, but they will always be related closely to the work you have been doing in the workbook. Each year the question will be about identity and comes in two parts, each taking the form of a short essay. The first part will ask you to show the progress you have made in developing one of the key social science skills: understanding how social science arguments are constructed. The second part will give you an opportunity to explore some of the key framing questions and debates of Block 1.

 You might find it useful to have a quick look at the *Assignments Booklet* before you start work on Block I, so that you have some idea of what you are looking for before you begin your study of *Questioning Identity* and this workbook.

You already have quite a lot to go on to guide your reading of Block 1: keep in mind the three framing questions and the first key skill, the production of knowledge in the social sciences. It might be useful to keep in mind the grid below as you work through Block 1 as a way of collecting your thoughts on these issues from across the four main chapters of *Questioning Identity*.

 Now read Kath Woodward's Introduction to *Questioning Identity* and listen to Audio-cassette 3, Side A: *Block I Overview*. Then return to this point in the workbook.

Framing questions of Block 1

	Chapter 1	Chapter 2	Chapter 3	Chapter 4
How are identities formed?				
What control do we have over our identities?				
Uncertainties about identity. Evidence of diverse identities.				
How is social science knowledge produced?				

1 QUESTIONS OF IDENTITY

We now come to the first chapter of *Questioning Identity* and in it Kath Woodward starts exploring what identity actually means (Sections 1 and 2). She goes on to introduce you to some of the key social scientists who have developed ideas about identity in their work (Sections 3 and 4). Then she uses those ideas to open up and explore some case studies of uncertain and changing identities (Sections 5–8). At the same time the chapter begins to think about what constructing a social science argument involves and how we can begin to judge the kinds of knowledge and argument that social scientists generate.

Chapter 1, 'Questions of Identity'.

- Understanding what social scientists mean by identity.
- Identifying and understanding the key questions of the chapter.
- Recognizing the role of *concepts*, and *theories* in the ways social scientists construct their arguments about identity.
- Understanding DD100's model of the *circuit of knowledge*.
- Developing your writing skills.

 Now please read Chapter 1, 'Questions of Identity' and return to this point in the workbook. You should spend about two thirds of your time this week on Chapter 1 and the rest on this section of the workbook.

1.1 Identity. What is it?

How did you get on with reading Chapter 1? Could you identify the main issues? Did you remember to start by asking yourself some questions? You could also have used the questions in the chapter to structure your reading.

If you think you need more help with *active reading* look back to the advice in Section 3 of the *Introductory Workbook*.

WORKBOOK ACTIVITY 1.1

As a way of checking your understanding of Chapter 1, can you pick out the main features of identity?

COMMENT

Most of the key features of identity were outlined in Sections 1 and 2 of the chapter. We listed:

identities combine how I see myself and how others see me

identity links the personal and the social

- identities are established by similarity and difference
- identities can be seen as fixed or fluid, individual and collective
- we have multiple identities
- identities have to be adopted, we have to take up identities actively.

These features combine to produce a *concept* of identity; not just yours or mine, or ours, but what it means to talk about identity in general. What can we do with this concept? Let's try using it to address one of the framing questions posed in Chapter 1.

WORKBOOK ACTIVITY 1.2

Is there uncertainty about identity in the contemporary UK?

What evidence does the chapter offer of uncertain identities? What particular examples are used?

COMMENT

Chapter 1 offers several different examples of uncertainties. Section 4 considers changes in social structures, including those of class, gender and culture and Section 6 explores the specific case of economic changes resulting in the loss of jobs and changes in communities using John Greaves's writing about his own experience. The Jackie Kay poem in Section 7 looks at challenges to traditional ideas about national identities, for example about being British or Scottish and the racism that may be one response to ethnic diversity. Section 8 cites examples of body projects, new social movements and new technologies and cultural practices, all of which can be seen to challenge old certainties about the limitations of the body and the social and cultural meanings that are given to the body.

How can we link the general concept of identity with particular examples of uncertainties about identity? The diagram overleaf is one take on this.

Can you see how we have taken features of the general *concept* of identity, linked them together in a way that both addresses the question and draws upon the examples? Using general concepts to compare or encompass a range of individual examples is an important element of constructing a social science argument.

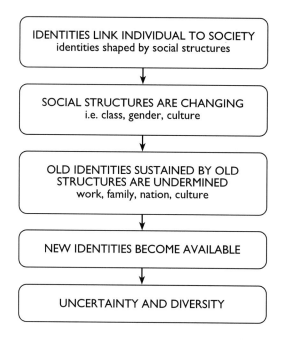

1.2 Constructing social science arguments

In Section 1.1 we began to construct an argument by defining a general concept of identity and applying it to a range of individual examples – it helped us to organize our material. The next stage is to generate an explanation: concepts need to be organized and animated as a *theory*.

Our starting point is Chapter 1, Section 3 where you were introduced to a range of ways in which social scientists have attempted to answer two questions about identity: 'How are identities formed?' and 'How much control do we have in the construction of our identities?'

What concepts and what theories are at work here?

WORKBOOK ACTIVITY 1.3

Look at the list of words below, they are all drawn from Section 3 of Chapter 1:

giving off information

unconscious

imagining

roles

identification

symbolizing

performance

sexuality

actors

Can you note down which of these concepts is used in the work of Mead (Section 3.1), of Goffman (Section 3.2) and of Freud (Section 3.3)?

C O M M E N T _____

There is some overlap, but the concepts are mainly used as follows:

Mead: imagining, symbolizing.

Goffman: actors, roles, performance, giving off information.

Freud: identification, sexuality, unconscious.

Crudely put concepts are grouped together to produce theories and theories should generate explanations, as in the diagram:

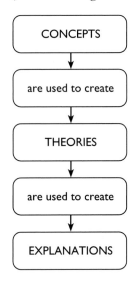

We are going to use the model above to follow through the works of Mead, Goffman and Freud and to illustrate the process involved in the construction of explanations and arguments from concepts and theories.

WORKBOOK ACTIVITY 1.4

We will start with Mead. The key concepts in Chapter 1 are imagining, symbols, symbolizing and visualizing.

How can these concepts be put together to generate a theory?

C O M M E N T _____

According to Mead, in order to have an identity and to know 'who we are' we have to be able to imagine ourselves. We do this through symbols. We see pictures of ourselves in our own minds. This means that ideas, images and symbols are central to Mead's theory of identity. They are more important than the bodies we inhabit or our economic circumstances. This explanation of how identities are formed emphasizes what goes on in the heads of individuals and the use of images and symbols in the process of visualizing themselves when people decide who they are. Given this starting point what social scientists need to investigate is: what are the symbols which people use to imagine themselves?

Mead's explanation suggests that people have some degree of control over the identities which they adopt.

Let us try going through the same process with Goffman's and Freud's approaches, but this time we will represent the argument diagrammatically using the framework set out above.

Goffman on identity

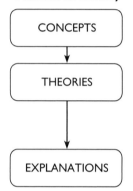

CONCEPTS — Roles, actors, performance, giving off information.

THEORIES — Identities are acted out in everyday interactions with other people. We act out identities rather like parts in a play, where the scripts are already written, but we have some scope for giving our own version of the parts we play.

EXPLANATIONS — Identities are social, the product of the society in which we live, but people can convey information about themselves and gain information about others, about who they are, through the way people behave with each other. People are not always conscious of how they play their parts but there is some possibility of individuals interpreting their roles. We can find out about how this happens by observing everyday interaction.

Freud on identity

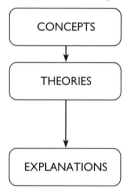

CONCEPTS — Unconscious, identification, childhood experience, sexuality.

THEORIES — Freud's psychoanalytic theory argues that identities are formed unconsciously as well as consciously; early childhood experience is important in shaping the people we become as adults; identities are fragmented and changing.

EXPLANATIONS — In order to understand identity formation in individuals we have to explore their early childhood experience and the way in which they may have repressed desires into their unconscious. It is also important to think about how individuals' gender and sexual identities are formed through childhood.

1.3 Sources of identity: writing skills

In this section we want you to try and use some of the concepts, theories and explanations developed in Chapter 1 in a short piece of writing: a mini-essay. First a few basics on essay writing in the social sciences.

1.3.1 Four golden rules of essay writing

1   Write the answer in your own words

This means that, however tempted you may be, or however much better the book you are using may seem compared with anything you could write, you have to avoid *plagiarism*. You can quote from an academic source, giving full details and using quotation marks, but you must never pass off someone else's words as your own. (See the *Introductory Workbook*, Section 8.4.) Make notes in your own words. This will help you understand the argument and use your own words when you write up an essay.

2   Answer the question asked

Spend some time thinking about what the question is actually asking. Pick out the key words and make sure you answer the question set (and not one you wish was there!).

3   Organize your material into a coherent structure

In most cases you will have to be selective. Remember the reader does not know what is on your mind so you will need to take the reader – your tutor – through the essay, making clear what you want to say and signposting each stage in the argument. For a clear structure see rule 4.

4   What a social science essay looks like

Title	Write out the title clearly, in full, at the start of the essay.
Introduction	Say what your intentions are in this essay.
Main section	Develop the key points you want to make and cite the relevant evidence to support them.
Conclusion	Sum up what you have said and make a final statement in response to the question set.
References/ bibliography	List the publications you have referred to in the essay.

We will come to more detailed guidance on social science writing in Sections 6 and 7 of this workbook. For the moment we want you to have a go using the outline above. After the title you'll probably want no more than one or two sentences for your introduction and one or two sentences for your conclusion, leaving you, in this activity, about 100 words for your main section. Make sure you include some evidence in the main section to back up your argument and *do* make sure that you reference your work.

WORKBOOK ACTIVITY 1.5

We would like you to choose one of the questions below and write a short piece, about 150 words (and no more), about the one you choose. The questions focus on particular aspects of identity illustrated in Chapter 1.

Question 1. In your own experience how is work linked to identity?

Here are some ideas on what you need to think about in order to answer this question.

What sort of work do you do – or did you do? Paid or unpaid? Where is/was the work done? A brief description would set the scene.

Next you need to think about the links. Go back to the definition of identity and try turning some of the features of identity into questions about the work you do. Work offers a useful example of the link between the personal and the social. The kind of paid work we are able to do, or are prevented from doing, is very dependent on social structures. How much control do you have over your work identity? Do others define you by the work you do? Do you do this work with others? Is there a sense of belonging to a community (as in the Greaves example) where this work is done? Do you consciously share this identity with others?

How important is your work-based identity to you? Are there contradictions between this identity and other identities you have?

Question 2. What is the link between place and identity in your own life?

This could be the place where you now live or the place you come from. It could be a region or a country or a particular type of community. The Jackie Kay poem illustrates the importance of place, especially in relation to how we see ourselves and how others see us. Place may have particular importance in relation to ethnicity or national identity.

Do you *identify* with the place you come from or the place where you live? Is the identity associated with this place in any way distinctive or different? How do you see yourself and how are you seen by others in relation to this identity?

Question 3. How are identities represented?

This option is a bit different from the other two. Look at the Age Concern poster in Chapter 1, Section 8.1. Now pick another example of your own, for example a picture of a person from an advertisement in a magazine or newspaper. It could be the successful young professional, the street-wise teenager, the anxious mother, the good mother, the caring father. Choose one that has a clear message and which might seek to hail or interpellate a particular type of identity.

What identity is being represented? What *symbols* are used to produce meanings about this identity? Who do you think is being invited to identify with this identity and to what purpose?

There will be more opportunity to develop these skills when you get to *Study Skills Supplement 1: Reading Visual Images* and you will do more work on this with Chapter 4, but make a start here.

1.4 Social science and the circuit of knowledge

So far we have thought about the practical nuts and bolts of constructing an argument:

1   Clearly defined general *concepts* help us organize and think about particular examples of a phenomenon.

2   *Concepts* can be combined together to generate *theories* which are general frameworks for providing explanations of phenomena.

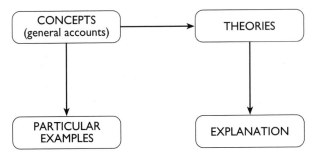

But how do we begin to examine and evaluate the quality of those concepts, theories and explanations?

You may recall from our discussion of the progress of the argument in the *Introductory Chapter* (see Sections 2–4) that:

● Social science enquiry starts with questions.

● Evaluating answers to these questions requires us to sharpen up our argument. We need to generate specific claims, descriptive or explanatory, that are fit for rigorous exploration.

● Social scientists reach for evidence when examining these kinds of claims.

● Evidence does not speak for itself – but must be carefully handled, sifted and interpreted.

● This process is broadly what we call *evaluation* – a process which often generates new questions to be resolved as well as confirming or contradicting the original claims.

In DD100 we have linked these processes of enquiry together in what we call the *circuit of knowledge*, see Figure 3(a).

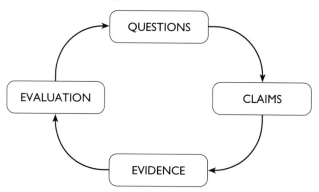

FIGURE 3(a) The circuit of knowledge I

You will find later in DD100 how concepts, theories and the arguments one can construct out of them also shape the way we use evidence and do our evaluation. But for the moment just think about concepts and theories as a way of generating descriptive and explanatory claims, see Figure 3(b).

Let us see how it works in a bit more detail in Chapter 1.

Questions

Chapter 1 began with three framing questions.

How are identities formed?

How much control do we have in shaping our own identities?

Are there particular uncertainties about identity in the contemporary UK?

In order to begin answering these big questions the chapter tries to focus on more specific manageable claims. Kath Woodward picks out areas of identity which might be particularly important. We will focus on issues of work and work-based identities.

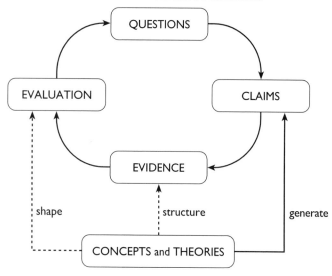

So we can rephrase our questions as:

How are work-based identities formed?

How much control do we have over work-based identities?

Are there uncertainties about work-based identities in the contemporary UK?

What claims does Chapter 1 make in response to these questions and how do concepts and theories of identities developed in Chapter 1 help us generate those claims?

FIGURE 3(b) The circuit of knowledge II

Claims

Drawing specifically on the arguments of Mead, Goffman and the accounts of social structures in Section 4 of Chapter 1, we picked out these claims.

- Work-based identities are formed by the interaction of individuals with economic structures which generate a repertoire of roles, symbols and conventions that individuals take up and identify with.

- Individual control over work-based identities are structured, patterned and constrained by the pre-existing conditions of work and distribution of economic opportunity.

- Individuals may have more choice over whether they choose to identify with work-based identities than other identities such as gender or place.

- For men who have worked in traditional industrial sectors, work-based identities have become more uncertain.

Evidence

The next step Kath Woodward takes is to look for some information against which these kinds of claims can be tested.

John Greaves's autobiographical account offers one type of evidence about the importance of work and identity. This piece suggests that structural changes in the economy can have significant impacts upon identities.

WORKBOOK ACTIVITY 1.6

Look back at your notes on Section 6.

1 What does John Greaves's writing tell us about how identities are formed?

2 How much control did he have in shaping his work-based identity?

3 Does his account suggest that there is greater uncertainty about work identities in the late 1990s?

COMMENT

1 John's account suggests that paid work, especially in work like coal mining, is a very important dimension of identity. Miners lived in a community dominated socially and economically by the coal industry. There is a strong connection between personal experience and the social factors related to paid work, and a strong sense of belonging – of being the same as others within the community.

2 Within coal mining communities there was little room for the expression of alternative identities to work-based ones – for men at any rate, so all-encompassing was the place of coal mining in the life of the community. External social forces that brought about the collapse of the mining industry clearly had, and still have, significant impact on the identity of John and those who live in his community.

3 This account does suggest there are greater uncertainties about identity, especially work-based identities in the coal industry (and other heavy manufacturing industries) in the UK. This is illustrated by the irony of the old Coal Board slogan 'A Job for Life'. For many people like John, who had expected that to be the case, they were left not only without a particular job, but without any job, in a community which had been prosperous and was, by the late 1990s, impoverished.

The activity above begins to explore the relationships between asking questions and making claims and using evidence. However, you are probably already thinking of some more questions which we could be asking about our example of the link between work and identity. In particular, one person's account might not be representative of the UK as a whole, or even coal miners in general. We need more *quantitative* evidence; especially to address the question about greater uncertainty in relation to changing social structures.

The evidence we have looked at so far is qualitative and provides significant insights into the personal side of the identity equation. It takes on board personal feelings as well as conveying the sense of community at two different moments in time, but it would be useful to know more about the scale of pit closures and of alternative employment which might have become available, for example. Is this story only about men? The community John describes is one peopled by women, men and children. What might be missing from this account?

Evaluation

How far have we gone around the circuit of knowledge? We started by focusing our general framing questions into more specific work-identity related questions. We drew on theories of identity to generate specific, sharper claims and looked at one piece of autobiographical evidence.

However, as we evaluate the original claim, in the light of evidence available to us, we might need to consider some more questions. What else do we need to know? What would more quantitative evidence about economic change and employment add? John Greaves's story is an account of a changing work-based identity but it is also a gendered account. It would also be interesting and useful to find out about the experiences of women in the community and whether a changing work identity had an impact on gender identity too. By comparing the work, paid and unpaid, and home experiences of women and men we might come up with a different set of claims about identity. We started with questions and the investigation has led to the addition of more questions as we complete our circuit of knowledge (see Figure 4). This leads us to Chapter 2, which asks more questions about gender and gendered identities.

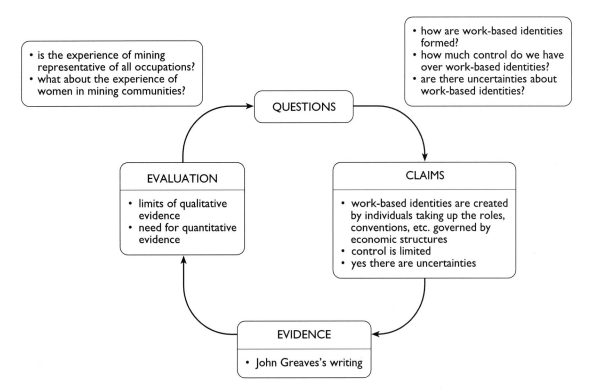

FIGURE 4 The circuit of knowledge with comments based on our work on Chapter 1

2 IDENTITY AND GENDER

In Chapter 1 you looked at three sources of identity: the work we do, the places we come from, and our bodies and biology. Each of these sources of identity offered both the promise of certainty in a changing world and causes of new uncertainties and contradictions.

The three chapters that follow each focus on just one of these sources of identity. In Chapter 2 we look at how far our identities could be influenced by our biology and ask: by what mechanisms and processes might our genes or our bodies determine who we are? Whether we are male or female, old or young, able bodied or disabled, what kind of social consequences flow from these embodied origins?

The authors of Chapter 2, Jenny Gove and Stuart Watt, begin by thinking about how biological and social structures are entwined in shaping gender identities (Sections 1 and 2). They go on to explore how children learn to recognize gender identities (Section 3) and take on gender identities themselves. They then take just one of many current issues to illustrate these debates: the differences in educational achievement between boys and girls (Section 4). This provides an opportunity to unpack how a social science argument is constructed. In working through these arguments, they will also look in more detail at the types of evidence social scientists draw upon, and some of the skills required for working with numbers and gathering evidence in the social sciences.

KEY TASKS

Chapter 2, 'Identity and Gender'.

- Understanding some social science accounts of gender identity and its entwined biological and social origins.

- Understanding what psychologists mean by stereotypes, categorization and cognitive development, and how they use these concepts to explain identity formation.

- Recognizing some of the methods of research used by psychologists.

- Reading simple arithmetical material relating to educational achievement and describing the patterns it shows.

- Being able to take a social science argument and show how it has been constructed. (In this case one relating to educational achievement and identity.)

Please read Chapter 2, 'Identity and Gender' and return to this point in the workbook.

For this study week you should spend around two thirds of your time reading the chapter and the rest on this section of the workbook.

2.1 Chapter 2. What's it about?

WORKBOOK ACTIVITY 2.1

In order to check your understanding of the chapter we would like you to think how Chapter 2 addresses one of the framing questions of the book about identity formation. Look back at your notes and think about this question:

How are identities formed? In particular, what does Chapter 2 tell us about how gendered identities are formed?

Try organizing your response into a diagram which covers some of the different concepts and theories which the chapter offers.

COMMENT _____

We picked out the following concepts as important to the production of the key arguments in Chapter 2.

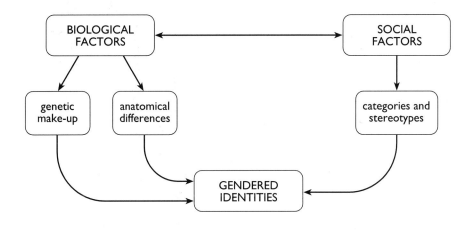

Gendered identities are usually classified as women/female or man/male. These categories are conceptualized differently by different social scientists and others. Some see them as fixed, essentialist categories. Others see more 'grey areas' and think of them as fuzzy or non-essentialist categories.

Section 3 of the chapter suggests that the ways in which we define and use these categories is developed in childhood, but then changes as children seem to recognize, at first, simple anatomical gendered categories and then learn to recognize more complex social categories.

What we have called biological categories here include anatomical difference based on our bodies as well as our genetic make-up. Children begin by basing their understanding of gender identities on fixed, essentialist, notions of difference that are linked to social stereotypes. This process begins through self-categorization. As children grow up they learn a more complex, non-essentialist categorization of gender difference.

2.1.1 More about evidence

Chapter 2 draws on a range of different types of evidence: social and biological evidence used to allocate people to gender categories in Section 1, transcripts of children's conversations and accounts of role play in Section 3, and quantitative statistical evidence of educational performance in Section 4.

The type of evidence used by social scientists varies, as do the *methods* which they employ to obtain that evidence. For example, in Section 3, in studying the development of young children, psychologists have used direct *observational* methods, while Section 4 draws upon indirect statistical methods. The methods employed are influenced by the kind of evidence which social scientists seek to obtain, for example, whether that evidence is qualitative or quantitative.

In the next section we are going to look in more detail at using quantitative data as evidence. You might feel comfortable with such material, in which case you can skip Section 2.2, but if you feel anxious about dealing with numbers work through the material below.

2.2 Gender differences in educational achievement: working with numbers

The first half of Chapter 2 focused on how we construct gender categories and how children learn to use these categories. Now we come to the question of how far these gendered identities influence children's behaviour in schools and, specifically, their achievement in examinations. Until recently the dominant political concerns in this field were about girls' under-achievement in school. Recently the issue of boys' under-achievement has hit the headlines and boys' GCSE results have helped trigger these concerns.

Figure 2.5 of Chapter 2 is a bar chart which shows the GCSE results of girls and boys in different subjects. Bar charts are a very useful way to display information, so let's pause here a moment and work through the skills involved in reading this one. (Part of Figure 2.5 is reproduced in Section 2.2.2 below.)

The figure is a bar chart showing results in percentages so there are two skills involved. One is understanding percentages, the other is reading bar charts displaying them. Let us start with percentages.

2.2.1 Percentages

Percentages are a very common and useful way to describe exact parts of something. The most common way to describe a part of something is to use forms like 'a half' or 'a quarter', but when you want to describe a part which is not a half, a quarter or a third, or you want to be very precise, then percentages are very convenient. They are used frequently in newspapers – and in social science courses.

This section of the workbook aims to ensure you really understand this useful idea. If you are sure you do, just do the exercises to check, but for many people percentages are a bit of a mystery; so here is a short introduction.

You recognize a percentage by the symbol %. It is read as 'per cent' and it means 'out of a hundred'. So, if out of 100 children in a room, 5 are girls and 95 are boys you can say that 5% of those in the room are girls and 95% are boys.

Things are not quite so straightforward if there are fewer or more than 100 children in the room. Then, in order to work out the percentages of girls and boys, we need to do some calculations. The calculations are worth doing because in the social sciences they offer an easy way to *compare* proportions when you need to do so. Let us see how this works.

WORKBOOK ACTIVITY 2.2

Suppose there are only 50 children in the room. 5 of them are girls and 45 are boys.

What percentage of the children are girls? Try to work it out for yourself first. If you do not know how, just read on.

COMMENT _____

10% of the children are girls. Here are a couple of ways of working that answer out. See which is clearer to you.

Out of 50 children, 5 are girls. To calculate the girls as a percentage of the total, we have to treat the whole group of 50 as if they were 100. We need to multiply by 2 to turn 50 into 100. Then we multiply the number of girls by 2 as well. 5 out of 50 is the same as 10 out of 100 or 10%.

Alternatively, we can state the proportion of girls as

$$\frac{5}{50}$$

Then to turn the fraction into a percentage, you just multiply by 100

$$\frac{5}{50} \times 100$$

You can work out the answer to that by hand or on a calculator. We advise a calculator! On a calculator, you first divide 5 by 50, then multiply the answer by 100. Try it now, and check that you get the answer 10.

By hand, you need to 'cancel' the fraction like this: first divide top and bottom of the first fraction by 5

$$\frac{5}{50} \quad \begin{matrix} \text{divide by 5} \\ \text{divide by 5} \end{matrix} \quad = \frac{1}{10}$$

then multiply the result by 100

$$\frac{1}{10} \times 100 = \frac{100}{10} = 10$$

You do not need to understand that calculation to work happily with percentages. The calculator method is just fine.

We can now turn that calculation into a rule:

Rule 1: Calculating a percentage. To express one number as a percentage of another, divide the first number by the second and multiply by 100.

WORKBOOK ACTIVITY 2.3

Check your understanding of this rule by using a calculator to answer the following:

1 You get 42 marks out of 70 for an assignment. What is your mark as a percentage?

2 In an (imaginary) UK opinion poll in 1999, 2,500 people were asked who Gordon Brown was. 425 did not know. What percentage had never heard of the Chancellor of the Exchequer?

3 In a group of 325 people, 65 own a computer and 52 have access to one at work. Express that statement in percentages.

COMMENT

1 60%

2 17%

3 20% own a computer and 16% have access to one at work.

2.2.2 Reading bar charts

Now let us return to the bar chart and have a careful look at this way of displaying information. Bar charts are really good at showing quantitative data in ways which allow the reader to absorb and understand them. They are worth a bit of effort to get used to them. We are not going to worry here about drawing them, just reading them.

Reproduced here as Figure 5 are just two parts of Figure 2.5 from Chapter 2: the results for English and Maths, for girls and for boys. Start by reading the title: it says these are results for 16-year-olds showing the percentage of girls and the percentage of boys achieving GCSE results A*–C.

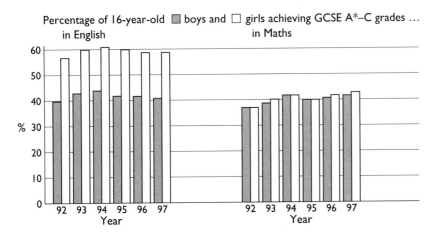

FIGURE 5   Bar chart of girls' and boys' GCSE results
Source: *The Observer*, 4 January 1998

Now look at the *axes*, that is, the horizontal line across the bottom and the vertical line up the left-hand side. Read the labels on these axes carefully. The vertical one shows the percentages defined in the title, from 0 up to 60%. The horizontal axis reads '92', '93' ... '97', so this shows a series of years. The chart is going to show percentages for each year, so we can look at changes over time. Finally there is a *key* or *legend*: this tells us which of the bars for each year refers to girls, and which to boys.

WORKBOOK ACTIVITY 2.4

Look first at the English GCSE part of the bar chart. Explain in words what it shows, without looking back at the chapter.

COMMENT _____

It shows that girls have consistently done better than boys, and that this has not changed a great deal. Around 60% of girls achieved A*–C grades each year from 1993 to 1997, and a slightly lower percentage in 1992. Only about

40% of boys managed the same grades in 1992 and from 1995 to 1997, and somewhat more than 40% in 1993 and 1994. There is no trend: that is, the percentages are not consistently rising or falling over the six years.

WORKBOOK ACTIVITY 2.5

Now Maths: what does it show, and how does it compare with English?

COMMENT

In Maths, the performance of boys and girls is very similar. And there is a trend: results have been getting somewhat better over the six years. Comparing Maths and English, we see that boys produce very similar results in the two subjects – hovering around 40% obtaining A*–C grades in both. However, a higher percentage of girls do well in English than in Maths.

2.3 Murphy and Elwood: constructing a social science argument

Having identified some key differences in boys' and girls' GCSE results in the 1990s, Jenny Gove and Stuart Watt take you through a range of possible explanations. They look at biological and cognitive factors and a range of social factors. They focus on the arguments of Murphy and Elwood: that children's gendered identities lead them, in general, to tackle school-work differently and to perform differently in exams. Murphy and Elwood aim to provide an explanation of the different performances of girls and boys by building up an argument about the links between gendered identities and school performance. We now want you to use their account of Murphy and Elwood's argument to help you think further about how social science arguments are constructed.

Chapter 2 shows that three claims form the core of Murphy and Elwood's work.

- *Claim 1:* Boys and girls foster different interests, attitudes, and behaviours prior to attending school, which are then perpetuated within school.
- *Claim 2:* Feminine and masculine identities are perceived in particular ways by teachers, with consequences that may impinge on achievement.
- *Claim 3:* In their school-work, girls and boys draw upon the different interests and skills that they have developed through their gendered experiences.

How are these claims put together? How is the argument constructed?

Look back at your notes and think about what is involved in the first claim.

Claim 1

This claim draws upon the biological, cognitive and social arguments which were introduced in Section 2. The interaction between these different components in early childhood development are seen as maintained in the school context. What constitutes typically gendered behaviour draws upon stereotypical gendered characteristics.

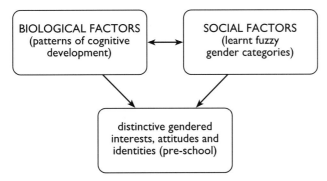

Claim 2

This claim argues that those pre-school attitudes and identities are reinforced by teachers, and lead to distinct gendered patterns of behaviour in skills with direct consequences for school performance and achievement.

Claim 3

This claim focuses on the cognitive skills which girls and boys have developed through their early childhood development. These skills directly impact on performance, though in different ways in different subjects.

The three claims combine to produce an argument which seeks to explain gendered behaviour and differential educational achievement in terms of an interaction between individual girls and boys and the social world which they inhabit. Typical gendered attitudes and attributes are reinforced and rewarded in the school setting so that children and young people develop and reinforce particular skills. Cognitive skills are developed and reinforced through social and educational experience. What is typical draws on gendered categories as discussed in Section 2. There is scope for reconstruction of categories here, and not everyone conforms, but the process is cumulative and interactive. It develops to include more factors and shows how gender identities are reinforced through an interaction between different interrelated factors, biological and social.

Thus the argument is both developed and expanded to include a range of evidence which supports the claims that are being made. The argument uses this evidence to show that biological factors, such as patterns of cognitive development, are closely linked to social factors, such as learned gender categories. These cognitive skills are developed both pre-school and subsequently at school, supported by the responses of teachers to children's pre-school development, creating a reinforcement of patterns of gendered performance.

3 IDENTITY, INEQUALITY AND SOCIAL CLASS

We started in Chapter 1 with an overview of the question of identity, its multiple forms and origins. In Chapter 2 we focused on gender as a source of identity and explored the interrelationship between biological and social factors in identity formation. In Chapter 3 we are going to consider a second source of identity: material and economic circumstances and look at class as a way of exploring this relationship. How important as a source of identity are our incomes, the jobs we have, the class we belong to, or what we spend our money on? Is class, in particular, still of key importance in deciding who we are and how others see us? Have the certainties once associated with class disintegrated and if so what, if anything, is replacing them? Engaging with these questions will require you to build on some of the skills you have already practised – using numbers, interpreting meanings and constructing arguments.

KEY TASKS

Chapter 3, 'Identity, Inequality and Social Class'.

- Understanding the kinds of questions social scientists ask about poverty, income and class, and their relationship to identity.

- Understanding how these questions can address the course themes of *uncertainty and diversity* and *structure and agency*.

- Using numerical data to describe income inequalities in the UK today and the way these inequalities are changing.

- Acquiring an understanding of the writings of Marx and Weber on class divisions and identities in society and being able to compare the ideas of Marx and Weber.

- Acquiring an understanding of the role of economic consumption in forming identities.

- Working further around the circuit of knowledge looking at the assessment and evaluation of claims and the role of comparison as part of this process.

Now please read Chapter 3 and then return to this part of the workbook. You should spend about two-thirds of your time working on Chapter 3 and the remaining time on this section of the workbook.

3.1 Getting orientated: economics and identity

When you finish working through a chapter it is worth seeing whether you can quickly draw together the strands of its argument. If nothing else it should help make clear to you the links or the arguments you are unsure about and identify areas that will need more work as you go through the workbook.

WORKBOOK ACTIVITY 3.1

Skim through your notes on Sections 1, 3 and 4: how could you represent the relationship of the key concepts and links in the chapter in note form or diagrammatically, above all the relationships between economic structures and identities?

COMMENT

There are lots of ways of doing this. We took the argument of Section 1 as the core of the chapter and put the key points into a diagram as follows.

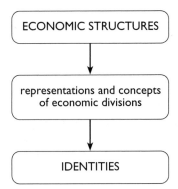

But what economic structures? Section 3 emphasizes the importance of paid work – the jobs we do, and Section 4 emphasizes the importance of financial wealth. Paid work and financial wealth are unequally distributed and generate inequalities in income (Section 3) and power (Section 4). So we could expand our diagram like this.

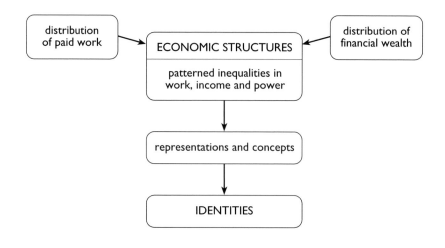

Chapter 3 looks at a number of different ways in which social scientists and the public in general represent or conceptualize those patterned inequalities. Sections 2 and 4 look at notions of poverty and wealth, Section 5 looks at Marx's and Weber's theories of class and changes in the structure of work. Section 6 looks at two accounts of the role of economic consumption in determining identity in the work of the sociologists Peter Saunders and Pierre Bourdieu and Section 7 looks at changes in patterned inequalities of income and power (social polarization) and a new attempt to represent and conceptualize its consequences for identities (social exclusion).

The key debates within this field are:

● which theory of class best copes with changes in the structure of work?

● which approach best explains inequalities?

● have class identities, as economic structures change, become less central and certain; what other economic identities, if any, are replacing them?

WORKBOOK ACTIVITY 3.2

How could you expand the diagram above to include some of the different explanations of identity in Chapter 3?

C O M M E N T

We tried this.

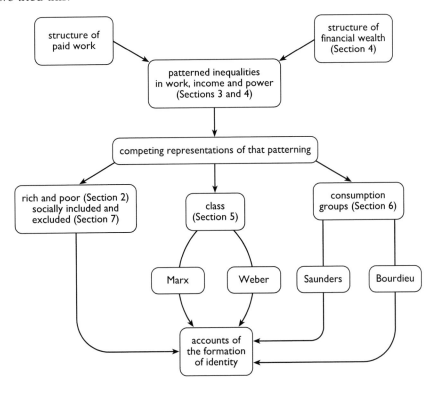

We're going to look at economic change, class and consumption identities in more detail later. Why do the authors of Chapter 3 focus on these? Why do the concepts of the 'poor' and 'socially excluded' not translate into economic identities?

W O R K B O O K ACTIVITY 3.3

Being poor is something we might expect to have important implications for the way a person sees himself or herself; to be a clear source of identity. As Section 2 makes clear this is not the case. Why not?

Do people who are *socially excluded* posses a culture and identity that are different from the mainstream?

Jot down some notes now from your reading of Sections 2 and 7.

COMMENT _____

We noted:

- There is disagreement over what we mean by poverty and how we define it. Poverty means different things to different people. Politicians and those on low incomes disagree over the meaning of poverty.

- Poverty is relative. How poor you are depends on what others have and what others expect.

- Poverty is seen to carry a stigma and, as the last paragraph in Section 2 makes clear, many of those who might be categorized as poor do not see themselves in this way at all. Being poor is a label which can be resisted or challenged or rejected.

- Jordan's research, quoted in Section 7, suggests that people who are socially excluded have values and aspirations which are very similar to the rest of society.

_____

This section of the workbook focuses on the ways in which patterned inequalities are linked to class structures in the generation and reinforcement of class-based identities. We start with inequalities. What do we mean by patterned inequalities? What sort of factors are included? These are some of the questions with which we might start an examination of class and identity. The questions create the need to look at what evidence we can find. The evidence, which is explored in Chapter 3, suggests that new occupations, new forms of consumption and other resources, such as pensions, are all relevant. The changes in these economic inequalities lead to claims about new class relationships and to new patterns of consumption, which themselves create new questions. Do these changes make traditional identities more uncertain? Are new, diverse economic identities emerging?

In Section 3.2 we go on to focus on the skills you need to tackle debates on patterned inequalities in income and wealth. In Section 3.3 we work through the debates about class and the relationship between class structures and identities. In Section 3.4 we will tackle the issues of uncertainty and diversity in economic identity.

3.2 How unequal are we? Using numerical data

In Chapter 3, Section 3 you were introduced to the income parade. Engaging with this image of the income distribution required you to draw on the skills you developed in your study of Chapter 2 (see Section 2.2 of this workbook). In addition, Chapter 3 asked you to think more about how to compare percentages and to think about averages. This part of the workbook offers more help with these skills. Once again, those of you who are confident of your numerical skills should skim this section and move on to Section 3.3.

3.2.1 Comparing percentages

One of the most useful things about percentages is that it allows you to *compare* proportions of *differently* sized populations. Let's make sure you understand just how such comparisons work.

Suppose in one local authority area the population is 300,000 people. Of these, 39,000 define themselves as black, 27,000 refuse to classify themselves, and the rest classify themselves as white.

In a second area, the population is 550,000. 60,500 classify themselves as black, 49,500 refuse to classify themselves, and the rest call themselves white.

WORKBOOK ACTIVITY 3.4

Which area has the higher percentage of people classifying themselves as white and as black? Which area has the higher percentage refusing to answer the question?

C O M M E N T

Area 1. By self-classification the population is 13% black, 78% white, and 9% refuse to answer.

Area 2. On the same basis, the population is 11% black, 80% white, with 9% refusing to answer.

So the first area has a higher percentage of black people, the second a higher percentage of white people, and the percentage of refusals is the same in both areas.

3.2.2 Averages

Chapter 3, Section 3 uses the idea of average household incomes. Are you happy with the idea of an average? This exercise helps you to check.

WORKBOOK ACTIVITY 3.5

Three households, all containing two adults, one child and an elderly person, have the following annual incomes: £9,700, £11,400, £35,000. What is the average household income?

COMMENT _____

To answer the question, add up the incomes and divide by 3. The total of the three incomes in £56,100. Dividing by 3 gives an average household income of £18,700.

_____

A second rule of thumb then is:

> **Rule 2: Calculating averages**. To calculate the average of a list of numbers, first add up the numbers and write down the total. Then count the numbers in the list, and divide the total by the count.

Look back at the example of household incomes above. The *average* income is well above the middle income of the three. This is because there is a big gap between the first two incomes and the third. So when you average them, the top income pulls the average up above the other two incomes. This is the effect we saw in real life in the UK income parade in Chapter 3. Income distributions tend to look like this. There are usually a relatively small number of very wealthy people, and their incomes pull *average* incomes up above the income of the household half-way along the parade. The income of the household half-way along is called by statisticians the *median* income.

3.3   Understanding social class

At the core of Chapter 3 are two theories of class – theories with distinct sets of descriptive and explanatory claims which allow us to bridge the gap between patterned inequalities of work/income and identities. In this section of the workbook we are going to re-examine these theories and begin to evaluate and compare them.

WORKBOOK ACTIVITY 3.6

You will be doing a substantial amount of work on comparing theories later in the course (particularly in Blocks 4 and 5) so this is really just a first try at something which will become quite familiar to you. The grid below gives you the opportunity to think about the similarities and differences between Marxist and Weberian approaches to class.

Fill in the empty boxes as far as you are able. These are some of the core claims of the theories. Then look at the completed grid at the back of this workbook (p.67) to help with those boxes you found difficult.

_____

Marx and Weber

	Marx	Weber
What is the structural basis of class divisions?		
Is class the main division in society?		
How many classes are there in capitalist societies?		
What relationship exists between classes?		
How and under what conditions do class divisions generate identities?		

How can we begin to compare these two accounts of class? Which makes more sense of the relationships between economic structures and identities? Making that judgement takes us back to the circuit of knowledge.

What is the key question being addressed here?

One way of putting it would be: How well do Marx's and Weber's theories of class explain how economic structures generate class identities?

Now we need to sharpen up this question into examinable claims for both Marx's theory and Weber's theory. How would you condense their arguments into a claim? We came up with:

Marx	Unequal and exploitative structures of capital ownership define economic classes. That inequality generates class conflict and class-consciousness and the embedding of class identities.
Weber	Unequal and parallel inequalities in access to and power in the labour market define economic classes.
	Economic competition between classes generates loose class identities.
	Social status and collective organization both within and outside the economic realm create more entrenched identities.

The next step, as you will now know, is to search out some evidence. Look back at the call centre case study and Chapter 3, Activity 3.3 (Section 5.4) for an example of this.

The comment on Activity 3.3 of Chapter 3 begins the final stage of the circuit of knowledge: evaluating the two sets of claims in the light of the evidence and pointing towards some new questions that might be asked.

3.4 The decline of old certainties: the construction of an argument

The call centre case study illustrates the issues of uncertainty and diversity. Changing economic structures and technologies may be re-creating and re-inventing class divisions, or they may, in some circumstances, be undermining old identities and generating new ones in their place. This is stated explicitly in Section 6.

WORKBOOK ACTIVITY 3.7

Section 6 tackles the issue of uncertainty and class identities from a number of angles. How can we summarize the key points made in Section 6?

Have a go yourself.

If you are not sure where to start, try to construct your notes around the following questions:

- What are the core elements of the concept of class?
- What do we mean by the old certainties of class?
- What are the two ways in which it is argued they are being eroded?
- What evidence is cited of a move from collective to individualist identities?
- What are the two theories which argue that class identities have been displaced or transformed by divisions based on consumption?
- How can you sum up what the section is saying about the erosion of certainties?

COMMENT _____

We came up with the following.

We noted that class identities share two elements:

1 They are collective identities.

2 They are identities closely linked to economic stuctures and rooted in occupations (both Marxist and Weberian approaches).

Changes can be seen has having taken place in relation to each of these two elements: collective identities and occupations.

Section 6 identifies three social science arguments that support the claim these identities are eroding:

1 Goldthorpe *et al.* on Luton car workers

2 Saunders on consumption cleavages

3 Bourdieu on social significance of consumption in relation to class.

Each of these arguments suggests that traditional class-based identities are being challenged as the major source of identity and of inequality, and that we have to take into account other factors if we are to have a fuller understanding of patterned inequalities and social relations. Goldthorpe *et al.* argue that there has been a shift from collective class identities towards greater individualism, whereas Saunders, like Bourdieu, places greater emphasis on patterns of consumption, especially consumption cleavages in shaping identities. Bourdieu retains the concept of class but stresses the importance of consumption in relation to class, for example arguing that what we buy, creates meanings about who we are, for ourselves and in the eyes of others.

As well as clarifying your notes this kind of exercise takes you one step further in your understanding of how arguments are constructed. In Chapter 2 we looked at the argument presented by Murphy and Elwood to explain patterns of educational achievement. We saw how it could be broken down into a number of linked claims each supported by examples and evidence and each linked to the previous one in a clearly signposted way. In this case what we are working on is more complex. We have a number of separate arguments, all converging to make the same general point, that class identity is becoming less certain. The construction of each argument internally is exactly the same as for the Murphy and Elwood example, i.e. it consists of a number of general statements supported by examples and evidence all linked to each other and building on each other. Each of these arguments is now linked to other statements to present a larger, more complex and comprehensive argument.

WORKBOOK ACTIVITY 3.8

What accounts for these shifts? What helps explain the erosion of old class identities for each of these arguments? What evidence is presented in Section 6 in support of these arguments? How can we summarize these changes?

COMMENT

We made the following points:

Class identities are changing in terms of shifts that have taken place

- in the jobs people do and which are available

and

- in the move away from collective, class-based identities towards more individualistic identities.

These changes are explained by:

Goldthorpe - the greater individualism of working-class people, eg car workers and the decline in collective solidarities, has led to a rise in instrumentalism, adoption of middle-class lifestyles by working-class people.

Saunders - more emphasis on consumption is allied to greater individualism and public/private consumption cleavages, changes in class alignment and de-alignment, eg voting preferences.

Bourdieu – consumption reinforces differences between classes, greater stress on the role of consumption, production and ownership of production are not the only factors that shape class.

All offer evidence of erosion of traditional class identities.

So has the significance and certainties of class identities in the UK diminished? On balance Chapter 3 has delivered claims, arguments and evidence that point in both directions. Marxist accounts of call centres suggest class identities change but endure; accounts of the death of class may have been exaggerated. Weberian theories suggest that class identities may endure, but become more uncertain as they are criss-crossed by diverse alternative hierarchies and identities. Consumption may be one of these hierarchies, but as Bourdieu notes this may reinforce class differences and identities rather than extinguishing them.

Evaluation, as you can see, is a complex process of sifting evidence, examining the case for and against and generating new questions. For a more definitive answer we would want to look at more areas of work than call centres, gather more data on consumption and identity, and ask more questions of more people about their identities.

 Now read *Study Skills Supplement 1: Reading Visual Images* and listen to the associated audio-cassette (Audio-cassette 2). Then return to this point in the workbook.

4 'RACE', 'ETHNICITY' AND IDENTITY

The UK is a multi-ethnic society and race and ethnicity are vital parts of identity. In Chapter 4 Gail Lewis and Ann Phoenix focus on the ways in which race and ethnicity are part of who we are, of how we see ourselves and of how we are seen by others. In changing times ethnic diversity offers both new opportunities for shaping our identities as well as uncertainties about who we are. The framing questions of this chapter remain those that were set out at the start of *Questioning Identity*.

How are identities formed?

How much control do we have in shaping our identities?

Is there more uncertainty about our identities in the contemporary UK?

These questions are linked specifically to what we mean by racial and ethnic identities, starting with a discussion of what is meant by the concepts of 'race' and 'ethnicity'. Chapter 4 examines some of the arguments that have been put forward by social scientists to understand these aspects of identity. It looks at some of the changes that have taken place in the UK and at the importance of the emergence of new and changing identities in a multi-ethnic society. Some of these changes have also led to uncertainties about what it means to be British in contemporary life. This is also the focus of TV 01, *Defining Moments*, which uses the example of the ritual of a state funeral to examine two different moments in post-war British history, to consider how the experience of being British might have changed during this period. Audio-cassette 3, Sides A and B both address the block's framing questions and offer discussion of several examples of racialized and ethnicized identities and of different ways of thinking about the block's key questions. Chapter 4 takes up the defining features of identity that were mapped out in Chapter 1 and applies them in the context of race and ethnicity.

Chapter 4, '"Race", "Ethnicity" and Identity'.

- Exploring the terms 'race' and 'ethnicity'.

- Understanding the processes involved in the formation of identities and the concepts of racialization and ethnicization.

- Understanding some of the ways in which 'racial' and 'ethnic' identities are formed in relation to other dimensions of identity.

- Exploring the links between how we are seen by others and how we see ourselves.

- Exploring the extent and impact of some of the changes that have taken place in the UK in the post-war period and more recently.

- Understanding the importance of sameness and difference and the ways in which identities are marked, for example through how they are represented.

- Constructing an argument based on the central questions of the chapter.

Now please read Chapter 4, '"Race", "Ethnicity" and Identity' and return to this point in the workbook. You should spend about two-thirds of your time on Chapter 4 and the remainder with this section of the workbook.

4.1 Who are you and where do you come from? Race, ethnicity and identity

The starting point for this chapter is the way in which our identities are constructed in relation to how we are seen by others and how we see ourselves and that ethnicity and race are central to these processes. We have thought about this already in this block. In Chapter 1, Section 7, Kath Woodward used the poem *So You Think I'm a Mule* by Jackie Kay to explore the relationship between how we see ourselves and how others see us and how we might be allocated to an ethnic or racialized group. You might find it useful at this point to refer back to the relevant section of Chapter 1. The poem explores the way in which a white woman classifies Jacky Kay by her visible appearance as a black woman, insisting that she cannot *really* be Scottish or British. The white woman's categorization of Kay is that she must be 'other' because she doesn't 'look' British.

What more general points can we draw from the poem which relate to the concerns of Chapter 4? We noted these points:

1 We are often defined by how others see us and how others impose an identity on us in relation to pre-given categories of race and ethnicity.

2 Such identities can be based on stereotypes which rely heavily on visible marks of difference.

3 Taking up an identity or having an identity imposed upon us are part of a *process*; identities are not fixed and given for all time.

4 Britishness, or Scottishness in this case, are assumed to be white, but whiteness is not explored.

5 Stereotypes and classifications can be rejected; we can choose to define ourselves.

The incident that is described in the poem is also about changes that are taking place in what it means to be British, which the white woman in this scenario seems not to have taken on board. What sort of changes are these? Have we changed our understanding of what we mean by race and ethnicity?

WORKBOOK ACTIVITY 4.1

Look back at your notes on Activity 4.1 in Chapter 4, at your understanding of the terms 'race' and 'ethnicity'. Then review these in the context of your work on Chapter 4. Has the use of these words changed? What changes have taken place in the lives of people in the UK in recent years which relate to these shifts? How do these changes make the terms racialization and ethnicization more useful than 'race' and 'ethnicity'?

COMMENT

Just as Kay in her poem takes a political position in response to how she is seen from outside, and seeks to define her own identity, Chapter 4 describes a range of changes, largely through collective action, whereby black and Asian people have sought to redefine their own identities. For example, Chapter 4 describes campaigns such as 'Black is Beautiful' and the activities of political movements where people have sought to take control of their own identities and to challenge racism.

The word 'ethnicity', or perhaps more commonly the term 'ethnic', is often associated with those who are not British or not white or even with some exotic outsider, as if white people did not belong to an ethnic group. This is a common usage in everyday speech, in the sale of goods and services, in restaurants, supermarkets and clothes shops, where 'ethnic' is not used to refer to British or English items. 'Race' is often associated with some biological categorization and may seem to suggest a fixed identity that is rooted in an essential quality that cannot be changed. Gail Lewis and Ann Phoenix argue that the terms racialization and ethnicization, although they may seem a bit longwinded, are much more useful than the more familiar 'race' and 'ethnicity' because they each refer to a *dynamic* process.

- Identities are not fixed for all times, they change. The addition of 'ization' recognizes the dynamic of this process.

- The process involves a struggle, sometimes between how we see ourselves and how others see us.

- Identities are socially constructed, linking social structures and the degree of control that we are able to exercise in shaping our own identities. This too is a dynamic process.

- How we represent ourselves as well as how others read the ways in which we represent ourselves are part of the ongoing and changing process of social construction.

4.2 Culture and the representation of identities

How we represent ourselves and how we are represented are important parts of the processes involved in identity formation. The ways in which identities can be interpreted are often located within cultural assumptions. As is argued in Chapter 4, ethnicity includes shared cultural practices, although ethnicity is a more specific and focused term than culture, which is more wide in its applications; the terms ethnicity and culture are not interchangeable. Many social scientists, like the authors of Chapter 4, prefer to call a society such as the UK a multi-ethnic society although people also refer to the UK as a multi-cultural society. What do we mean by culture?

4.2.1 Culture

You have already come across the idea of culture in a number of places and guises in DD100, for example:

- The concept of *sub-cultures* and their relationship to crime in Section 4.4 of the *Introductory Chapter.*

- Culture as a key social structure shaping identity in Chapter 1, Section 4.2 of *Questioning Identity.*

- The role of culture and meaning in relation to poverty and identity in Chapter 3 of *Questioning Identity.*

- Symbols and representations are important aspects of culture, Chapter 1, Section 8, *Questioning Identity.*

You will come across the notion of culture throughout the course so it is worth pausing for a moment to unpack the term.

What do you understand by the term culture (skim through your notes if you want to)?

You might have come up with something like:

ideas

customs

images

art

language

beliefs

sub-cultures

popular culture

The concept of culture, as it is used in the social sciences, can encompass all of these things because at its broadest it refers to the realm of meaning – and meaning can and is produced in everyday conversations, in great works of art, and through popular culture by religious beliefs and rituals.

Social scientists, without assuming any one type of culture is better or more meaningful than another or more worthy of investigation than another, recognize that there is a great diversity of cultures, realms of meaning and belief in any one society, and that these cultures cluster around specific social groups and social practices. *High culture* is the domain of traditional and elite art forms; *popular culture* is the realm of mass consumption and commodified culture. *Dominant cultures* reflect the meanings of the powerful; *sub-cultures* reflect the meanings of the deviant or the marginal.

4.2.2 Reading visual images

Your work on this chapter and the rest of the book has involved not only reading words but looking at a whole range of other kinds of material: photos, posters, maps.

Look at the photo in Figure 6. Rituals play a crucial role in upholding and reaffirming national identities. Émile Durkheim (1915) argued that nations need the cohesion and unity which such rituals and their sense of the sacred, as opposed to what he called the profane matters of everyday life, afforded.

The Remembrance Sunday ceremony is a ritual which presents people with part of the story of the British nation. It is part of the narrative of what it means to be British. Because of the coverage and attention given to the event each year it is a ceremony whose significance may be recognized and understood by many British people, even if they do not respond to it in the same way.

FIGURE 6   The Cenotaph, Whitehall on Remembrance Sunday

WORKBOOK ACTIVITY 4.2

1   What are the symbols used in the picture in Figure 6? List what you can see.

2   What meanings are attached to what you can see in the picture? What do you associate with your list in 1? Who is represented and who is not?

3   Finally, it is this photo, or one very like it, which appears in most British newspapers in November. But could it have been constructed differently, with a different focus? What implications might this have for the meanings which are being communicated?

C O M M E N T

1   The kinds of words we came up with immediately were:

> flag, established religion, the church, male hierarchies, discipline, uniforms, men, especially men on display, spectacle, soldiers, grouping, differentiation, solidarity, a cross, armed forces, monument, whiteness (the people we can see are predominantly white)

This list depends on some interpretations of symbols. For example, we have noted down both cross and religion. We needed to understand what a cross stands for before we could get to religion. The cross also symbolizes a particular religion, that of Christianity, and not others. Similarly we needed to be able to interpret guardsmen's hats to the right of the picture to give us armed forces.

2   Your response will depend on your own experience and on whether you are familiar with some of these military symbols. This image conveys a powerful message. The message becomes more powerful once we introduce our own knowledge of the context of the ceremony. We could add: the two World Wars, the Gulf Wars, and the Falklands War. We could say more about the participants: men in positions of power, heads of state of Commonwealth countries, the Queen, the British Legion and the Church of England as the established church. The presence of dignitaries makes this a high-status occasion and an important ritual.

3   The photo is one you would expect to see of the Remembrance Sunday ceremony and it is constructed in such a way as to make sure the meanings we have picked up on are clear to people looking at it.

But it could have been constructed differently to convey different meanings:

- A focus on those who are excluded, for example by ethnicity or gender, would serve to emphasize different elements in the national story.

- A close-up of disabled young service men would be emphasizing just one part of the narrative.

- The juxtaposition of this kind of image with one of a soldier selling his medals, or of a current protest about British military actions overseas would convey yet another message.

4.2.3 Representing Britishness

Meanings about national identities, for example being British or English, are often created and reinforced through representations, symbols and rituals. The idea of belonging to a nation invokes particular ideas about who is included and who is excluded. Chapter 4 makes some distinctions between the nation and the nation-state and national identity. What do we mean by a nation?

WORKBOOK ACTIVITY 4.3

Which of the following, if any, are nations and which are nation-states?

Britain

England

Ireland

Northern Ireland

The Republic of Ireland

Scotland

Wales

The United Kingdom

C O M M E N T

- The only nation-states in the list are the United Kingdom and the Republic of Ireland.

- England, Scotland and Wales are commonly thought of as nations, but there is no English state, Scottish state, or Welsh state, at present.

- Northern Ireland, in formal constitutional terms, is part of the United Kingdom, but very few people would consider it a nation or describe themselves as Northern Irish. Some refer to it as a province, others as the six counties, others as Ulster. Some people who live there consider themselves Irish, others consider themselves British, and some see their identity as Ulster men or women.

- Some people consider Ireland (the whole island and its people) as a nation, irrespective of the border. Many Northern Irish Protestants would bitterly contest this.

- Some people consider Britain and its people (that is, the UK without Northern Ireland) to be a nation; some would contest this.

The point of this activity is not to answer the initial question definitively, but to show how complex and contested the idea of a nation is, and to show how there is no easy or automatic fit between nations and nation-states. To unpack this issue, we need some basic definitions. Let's begin with the idea of the state. For our purposes the state is a cluster of institutions which lay claim to ultimate legal and moral authority over a given territory and whose claim is usually backed up by the monopoly of legal force and legal violence within that territory. In the UK today, the state is made up of the government, parliament, Whitehall and its ministries, national quangos, local government, the army and police. We use the term the UK state as a shorthand for these governing institutions.

If you look at a political map of the world today you will see clearly-marked borders that separate states from each other. However, the existence of clearly-marked and agreed borders is actually a fairly recent innovation. For most of human history, whatever the claims of states and their rulers, borders have been indistinct and unmapped. The authority of states and their monopoly of force, rather than being uniform over a territory, have tended to be strong at the centre but peter-out into ungovernable border lands and peripheries. This was true of great imperial states such as Rome, and of feudal states such as England in the fifteenth century when the rule of law rarely extended to the far north of England, for example. Nation-states, which we

FIGURE 7
Europe, 1000 AD

see represented on today's political maps – with fixed borders and uniform internal rule – have only been created in the last few centuries in Europe and even more recently in most of the rest of the world.

What then is the relationship between nations and nation-states? One claim has been that all people living within the fixed boundaries of a nation-state and under its uniform rule constitute a single community of fate, bound together in a common destiny by allegiance to a single set of state institutions. This appears to work for France, for example. France is the nation-state, and the French are the nation of people who live within its boundaries and under its rule; although the Bretons in the north of France, and the Basques who live near the Spanish border might have something to say about this. This simple equation between nation and nation-state soon breaks down once you look at a wider range of examples. In the case of Ireland, the island is divided into the Republic of Ireland, which achieved independence from Britain in 1921, and part of the UK nation-state: Northern Ireland. There are, however, many Catholics living in

FIGURE 8
Europe, 1999 AD

Northern Ireland who consider themselves part of the Irish nation but who live under the rule of the UK state. Alternatively, Scottish or Welsh nationalists consider themselves to be members of the Scottish or Welsh nation, but live under the rule of the UK state.

These conflicts and differences exist because, in the end, the nation-state is a political and legal entity, but nations are cultural entities. They are communities of people who feel they possess the same identity by virtue of shared cultures, histories, languages; and the geography of those communities does not necessarily correspond to the geography of political borders. In this context we can understand nationalism as both a psychological and political phenomenon. On the one hand nationalism is a psychological and emotional attachment to a nation, a sense of belonging and identity. But, more often than not, this emotional attachment to a community of fate has become entangled with a political project – the idea that a nation should govern itself, that it should acquire a nation-state of its own which can protect and nurture the interests and identity of that nation. It is this, in part, which distinguishes nations from other shared cultures and identities (Guibernau, 1998).

4.2.4 Reading maps

Maps offer one form of representation which often includes the boundaries of the nation-state. They can also present a visual image of historical processes, showing us how the nation has evolved.

You will be using maps in your study of social science so it is worth practising extracting information from them.

WORKBOOK ACTIVITY 4.4

Look at the map in Figure 9; what light, if any, does it shed on the following question?

- Is the idea of an authentic ethnic British, English or Scottish nation tenable?

COMMENT

The map shows that during this period the idea of a singular, unified ethnic British, Scottish or English person was unintelligible. Scotland barely exists as a meaningful entity, divided between Picts, Scandinavians, invading Scots (from the island of Ireland) and Anglo-Saxon settlement as far north as the Firth of Forth. Similarly, look at the area that you would now think of as England. The post-Roman occupants were overrun by Angles, Saxons and Jutes from the European mainland and, across a significant swath, overrun again by Scandinavians. The Norman Conquest meant that whoever it was that lived in what is now England acquired a French-speaking elite of Scandinavian origin.

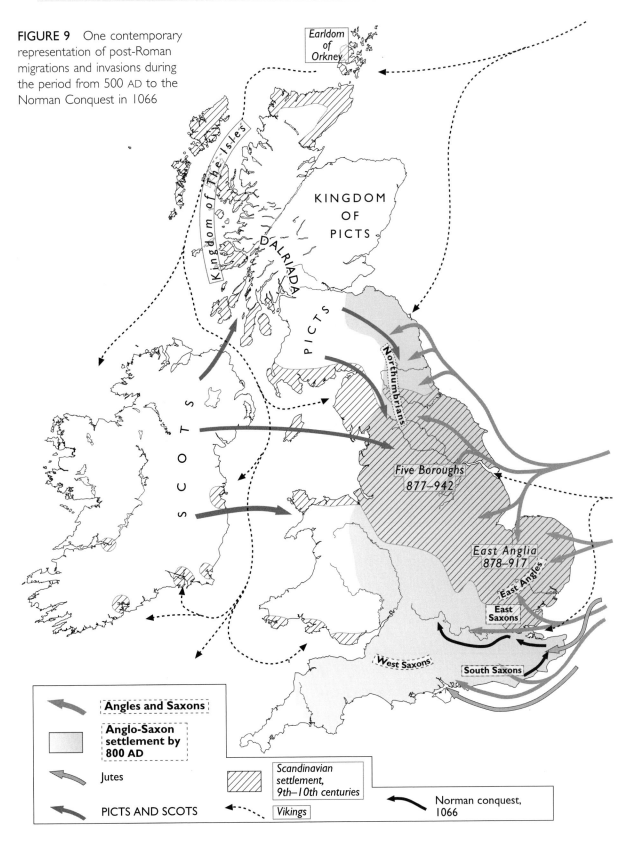

FIGURE 9 One contemporary representation of post-Roman migrations and invasions during the period from 500 AD to the Norman Conquest in 1066

4.3 The argument of Chapter 4: how is it constructed?

One of the tasks in this workbook is to look at how social scientists put arguments together. In this section we are going to go through the ways in which Chapter 4 constructs an argument by working through the different stages in this process. In order to do this we want to use the circuit of knowledge outlined in Figure 3(a) and address one of the central questions of Chapter 4:

> How are 'race' and 'ethnicity' important to our identities in the contemporary UK?

You will recall that the circuit of knowledge starts with questions, although the whole process is cyclical and each of the points on the circuit is linked to others.

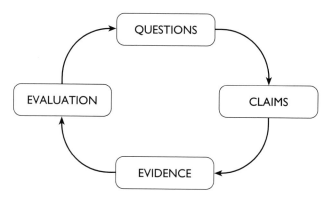

Chapter 4 offers discussion of a range of concepts that can be used to address this question. Concepts play an important part in the process of constructing an argument, as you have seen already in this workbook.

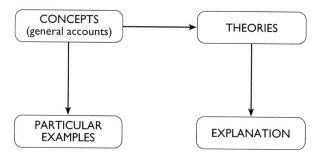

WORKBOOK ACTIVITY 4.5

What is the first stage in addressing this question? How would you start?

COMMENT

We suggest starting with an exploration of what we mean by the terms 'race' and 'ethnicity'. What do the terms mean? Chapter 4, Section 2 offers some useful discussion. In Section 2.1 you will have thought about your immediate response to these terms but Section 2.3 presents some more considered analysis of the ways in which these terms are used in the social sciences. Race can include some notion of biological and physical differences between people and many social scientists have employed quotation marks, 'race', to distinguish between a biological, fixed category and one that has political significance. Ethnicity includes cultural practices, religion and language. Gail Lewis and Ann Phoenix point to arguments about the ways in which racialization and ethnicization are preferred because of the ways in which these terms carry more of the idea of adopting an identity as a process, one that involves how we see ourselves and how others see us as part of an ongoing and often changing process.

WORKBOOK ACTIVITY 4.6

What evidence does Chapter 4 offer for the importance of ethnic diversity and racialization in the formation of identities in the contemporary UK?

COMMENT

The chapter offers a wide range of supporting evidence ranging from official inquiries, such as that into the murder of Stephen Lawrence, to personal testimonies. Chapter 4 cites examples of racisms that range from everyday insults to extreme acts of aggression as well as indicating importance of ethnicity and of ethnicization for everyone. Ethnicity is not something carried only by those who are black and Asian. There are no human beings who do not belong to an ethnic group of some sort. Section 4 looks at the ways in which those who might appear to be 'unmarked' are also shaped and influenced by the markers of ethnicity, for example in the discussion of different kinds of whiteness in Section 4.2. The discussion of the changing categories used in the Census in the UK, in Section 4.1.1, and the use of a range of different categories including, for the first time, sub-divisions of the white category in 2001 points to a recognition of both change in the formation of ethnicized identities and the centrality of racialization and ethnicization in the contemporary UK. Section 4 also explores popular cultural representation of ethnicized identities, for example what it means to be English or British.

WORKBOOK ACTIVITY 4.7

What claims are made in Chapter 4 about the centrality of racialization and ethnicization in the formation of identities?

COMMENT

Having established a range of supporting evidence the chapter makes a strong case for the argument that racialization and ethnicization are dynamic processes. They involve change over time and the need to recognize the specific circumstances in which identities are forged. This process involves a tension between how we see ourselves and how others see us. The categories through which ethnic and racialized identities are constructed can involve constraint from outside as well as agency, for example political movements which resist racist constructions of identity that are imposed upon people. These identities intersect with other identities and are not in some kind of separate category. Not only do they concern us all, an understanding of racialization and ethnicization is vital to our understanding of who we are in the contemporary UK.

WORKBOOK ACTIVITY 4.8

How can we weigh up these claims? What further questions do they raise?

COMMENT

The chapter offers a range of evidence of the impact of change, for example in relation to the diversity of identities that are available in the contemporary UK, which can be considered in relation to the uncertainties that are also manifest, for example in relation to what it means to be British or to be English at this historical moment. The course themes, including that of uncertainty and diversity, offer a useful framework for weighing up the claims made in the chapter. The theme of uncertainty and diversity is useful for describing and understanding the range of changes that have taken place. The theme of structure and agency is also to the fore in Chapter 4, especially in its coverage of the collective action that has led to new definitions of race and ethnicity and new claims about the processes that are involved in racialization and ethnicization.

These claims also inspire new questions about how we cope with change, about what kind of interventions are required to combat the negative effects of racisms as well as the ways in which we can categorize 'race' and ethnicity.

4.4 Conclusion

To sum up the argument we identified the following key points:

- Racialized and ethnicized identities are formed relationally, that is through being seen and seeing ourselves as the same as some groups of people and different from others.

- Notions of minority and majority are not just about numbers, they are also about power; those classified as a 'minority' are consequently marginalized and deemed to be less powerful and thus their interests are subordinated.

- Identities are fluid and changing, not fixed, and social scientists have to provide concepts and theories that can explain the dynamic processes involved in identity formation.

- Political struggles involve links between structures and the agency of groups and individuals.

5 CONSOLIDATION AND REFLECTION

As with the Introductory Block, we are going to round off our work on Block 1 by consolidating and reflecting on the materials we have worked through. The Afterword to *Questioning Identity* (as with subsequent books on DD100) begins the process of consolidation. Then the TV programme and Audio-cassette 3, Side B, give you more of a chance to reflect upon and explore some key issues in the block.

 Now read Kath Woodward's Afterword in *Questioning Identity* and return to this point in the workbook.

We hope you are beginning to establish for yourself what the most useful form of consolidation is for you.

One strategy might be to organize and condense your notes around a grid – look back to the Introduction of this workbook (p.9) where we set out one possible device for organizing your study of the chapters, based on the framing questions of the block.

Another closely related task would be to focus on two of the course themes as we have here – *uncertainty and diversity* and *structure and agency*. This is what we will do using the following grid.

WORKBOOK ACTIVITY 5.1

Try condensing some of your notes on a chapter by chapter basis on to the following grid – our version is at the back of the workbook.

 Now please listen to Audio-cassette 3, Side B and read the associated notes.

Also watch TV 01: *Defining Moments* and read the associated notes. Please check the *Study Calendar* for broadcast times.

Themes of Block I

	What uncertainties are explored in this chapter?	Why is diversity important in understanding these uncertainties?	How do we see people in this chapter shaping their identities?	What structures constrain and generate control over our identities?
Chapter 2				
Chapter 3				
Chapter 4				

6 STUDY SKILLS: USING TUTORIALS, THE PHONE AND SELF-HELP GROUPS

So far the emphasis has been on you, as an individual student, working by yourself with the course materials. However, you are not expected to work with the materials all by yourself unless that is really your choice. Even then there will still be quite intensive communications with your tutor in relation to your assignments. Learning from your assignments was touched on in Section 8.1 of the *Introductory Workbook* and is covered in more depth in *Workbook 2.*

What about the other kinds of support that are available to you as you work through the course and how can you be sure you are making the most of them?

Look at these four scenarios. Read each one and note down your response.

Scenario 1

You are slowly falling behind with your work on Block 1. You still haven't read Chapter 4 and you should be starting on TMA 01. There is a tutorial tomorrow. Should you go to it or spend the time catching up?

Scenario 2

You really don't understand part of Chapter 3. You have gone over it again and again and you can't see what Weber meant by a status group and now you realize part of the TMA is about this. Should you phone your tutor to ask for some advice or will this be wasting her time? You know she is very busy.

Scenario 3

At the first tutorial you found that one of the other students lives in the next road to yours. He suggests getting together to discuss the next TMA but you are worried that this might count as cheating. Will it?

Scenario 4

You know you are not going to be able to get to tutorials. Does this mean you should not have started the course or that the OU is the wrong place for you?

We want to start with scenario 4 because it is important to hear that the OU is committed to enabling people who would not be able to attend a conventional university to get degrees – so if you are not able to get to tutorials you must not let this deter you. We know that for some students attendance is not possible. If you are one of these students, your tutor will be able to put you in touch with other students studying the same course who may live near or be able to telephone you. You will be encouraged to keep in touch with the tutor yourself by telephone or letter, for students with disabilities special support can be arranged through your OU regional office.

Our response to scenario 1 would be that you should try to get to the tutorial. You will find that you are not the only person who is struggling to keep up. Your tutor will be ready for this and will be able to suggest ways of catching up. Let your tutor know of any difficulties. You will probably find that once you have mentioned a problem like this everyone else chimes in to agree with you. Don't be put off if some people in the group seem on top of their work. OU students vary enormously in terms of their educational experiences before starting a course and the time they have available to study the course. Remember, tutorials are not lectures. Come prepared to argue and ask questions, and listen to others. Doing this kind of work, often in small groups, leads to far better understanding and remembering, but it can take some getting used to.

If you are having a difficulty like the one in scenario 2, it is very important to phone your tutor. An important part of his or her job is to help students over the phone There are a few ground rules that will make this work better:

- if your tutor has told you already when are good times to phone, try to stick to these

- make some notes on the difficulty before you call, so that you can explain it clearly

- if you start getting confused whilst on the phone, and working like this does need a lot of concentration, ask the tutor if you can phone back when you have digested where you have got to.

With regard to scenario 3, discussing your TMA with another student can be very helpful indeed and certainly is not cheating. Your tutor will probably be encouraging you to form self-help groups: self-help can take the form of just calling each other for moral support but if you arrange meetings, try to have a definite topic to discuss. Remember though that when it comes to finally writing your TMA, the work must be all your own. This should not be a problem. Everyone has different ways of working through the ideas you have discussed. It is very difficult to produce the same piece of work as someone else.

7 ASSESSING BLOCK 1

It is now time to think about writing TMA 01. You have already covered a lot of ground on writing skills and learning from assessment.

- In the *Introductory Workbook*, Section 8, we covered the purpose of assessments (to help you understand the course) and the role of the workbooks in this (practising the skills you are assessed on).

- Section 1.3 of this workbook, as well as TMA 07, have given you a chance to practise writing.

- Section 1.3 also covered some basic ground rules for successful writing, and Section 8.4 of the *Introductory Workbook* introduced you to ways of referencing your writing.

In this section of the workbook we begin by answering some frequently asked questions about writing in the OU (Section 7.1), cover some guidelines for preparing to write (Section 7.2), and look at a few key points on the structure and purpose of TMA 01 (Section 7.3).

7.1 Frequently asked questions about essay writing for your TMAs

How closely do I need to follow the student notes? What if I want to answer the questions differently?

You received quite firm advice in the *Introductory Workbook* about using the student notes. In the early stages of the course, in particular, these notes will be detailed and will spell out for you very fully how to approach the question. If you find yourself wanting to do something very different it would probably be a good idea to stop and phone your tutor.

What kind of language should I be trying to use? Something like the language which is used in the chapters? Will this count as copying?

Another way of putting this might be: how can I manage to write in what sounds like an academic way without almost copying from the chapter?

This is not easy and it doesn't help to say it will come with practice. What you write can sound, as we have heard one student express it, very 'Janet and Johnish' compared to what members of the course team have written. Certainly if you are not sure exactly what something means it is easier to use the words in the chapter. However, copying is never acceptable and your tutor will warn you about this if it occurs. If you use the words of someone else you must reference them. Talking about the course ideas, as much as you can, to anyone who will listen – not just fellow students – and engaging with the ideas of the course will help you become more confident in using the language of the social sciences.

What about my own opinions and ideas? Can they be brought in at all?

Of course your own ideas and views are important: they will help you to engage with the course material. Using and testing those ideas are part of becoming an active and independent learner. The key issue is to subject your ideas and opinions to the same rigorous analysis we expect of social science arguments. You have already seen during your work on Block 1 that constructing and evaluating an argument in the social sciences involves quite specific components: clearly stated claims, systematic use of a range of evidence, clarity of concepts, etc. This can result in quite a different approach to issues and even a different style of writing from some kinds of journalism or from a discussion with friends or family. You may well find that an assignment task involves you in presenting an argument about something you have strong views on. You will need to construct the argument carefully, as a social scientist. You will need to pay attention to definitions, supporting evidence and internal coherence rather than relying on appeals to, for example, 'common sense' or what is 'natural'.

7.2 Preparing to write an essay

In Section 1.3 of this workbook you had a chance to practise writing skills and look at some key guidelines for good writing: use your own words, answer the question, organize your material, and use the conventional structure of introduction, main section, conclusion and references. In this section we will move on to how to organize yourself to achieve these ends. The key is planning.

Thorough preparation and planning is the basis of any good piece of written work. Here are some reminders for those of you already experienced in essay planning, and some suggestions for anyone coming to OU social science essay writing for the first time.

I   Look back

- If this is not your first essay, and if you haven't done so already, take a look at your previous one. Did your tutor make any suggestions that you need to bear in mind for this essay? Did you learn anything else about essay writing?

2　Read the question

- Identify the process or 'command' words like, *discuss, evaluate, explore.* These tell you how you have to answer the question. A list of these words and their definitions are covered in the Appendix at the end of this workbook.

- Identify the 'content' words. These tell you what you have to write about.

- Let's consider the question:

  Identities in the contemporary UK are becoming more uncertain. Discuss.

  'Discuss' is the command word. It implies that you have to explore the evidence for and against the statement. The content words are 'the contemporary UK' and 'uncertain'. So, the evidence that you need to explore should focus on whether there is increasing uncertainty about identities in Britain and you need to ask what 'uncertainty' might mean in this context.

3　Identify the relevant material

- Read the guidance notes that you get with each question. These will prevent a lot of unnecessary suffering and should always be consulted.

4　Organize the material

- Options include 'brainstorming' your ideas for the essay on paper: jot down a list of questions and issues prompted by the questions, all the relevant examples you can think of and any other related evidence; re-check notes and add left-out material; and then link connected ideas and points.

- Collate and write out these points on separate sheets of paper, on 'post-it notes', or on index cards.

- Shuffle these until you've got them in a logical order. **This is your essay plan**.

- Ideas may come to you at unexpected moments – for these keep a notebook handy and jot them down.

5　First draft to final version

- Working from your essay plan, begin writing a first draft. You may need to revise your plan as the essay takes shape. Don't worry, this is perfectly normal!

- Do the best you can, but see it as a first draft and expect to make some improvements. You may even want to prepare a second draft before writing the final version.

- We all know that people sometimes put their first draft straight in the post. If you have time, always put the essay aside for at least a day to let the dust settle, show it to a friend or another student to get feedback, and then re-read the question and the essay yourself. Its strengths and weaknesses should now be a lot clearer to you.

● You're now in a position to write your definitive answer. Now is the time to consider more carefully your presentation (sentence structure, grammar, etc.) and to check for clarity of expression.

● When this is complete, fill in your PT3 form, put the whole lot in the post and await your tutor's comments with quiet confidence.

In *Workbook 2* we will offer you more detailed help through the process of first draft to final version.

Essay planning has five principal stages:
● Reading and understanding the question.
● Identifying the relevant material.
● Making an essay plan.
● Writing a first draft.
● Reviewing the first draft and writing a final version.

7.3 TMA 01

TMA 01 is different each year, but it will have the same format and aims. It takes the form of two short essays, each on the subject of identity. You will find the question for this year with detailed advice in your *Assignments Booklet*. In this section we want to help you to think about the TMA and to show you how each section of this workbook has helped prepare you for doing it.

The first part of the TMA is asking you to show that you understand what is meant in social science by concepts, theories and explanations, evidence, and the way these are brought together to form an argument.

The second part of the TMA is where you are asked to present an argument using all such components.

At the end of the TMA there is another short exercise in self-assessment. You may find it useful to return to Section 8.3 of the *Introductory Workbook* to remind yourself of this exercise.

The subject matter of the TMA is, of course, about identity, but it is also asking you quite explicitly to show that you are able to use the skills we have been concentrating on in this first block, that is, how social scientists construct arguments. The figure below provides a summary of the way in which you have been building up these skills throughout your work on *Workbook 1*.

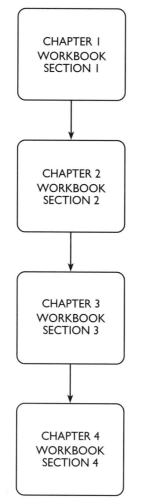

CHAPTER 1 WORKBOOK SECTION 1

Using general concepts to bring together many particular examples. Defining the concept of identity.

Using concepts to generate theories to generate explanations.

e.g. Mead, Freud and Goffman.

CHAPTER 2 WORKBOOK SECTION 2

Breaking down a social science argument into core claims and clarifying their interconnections.

e.g. the account of Murphy and Elwood of gender performance in schools.

CHAPTER 3 WORKBOOK SECTION 3

Comparing and contrasting arguments.

e.g. Marx versus Weber, class versus consumption.

Combining arguments.

e.g. accounts of the origins of uncertainty in economic identities.

CHAPTER 4 WORKBOOK SECTION 4

Using concepts and constructing theories.

Concepts of racialization and ethnicization. Supporting key claims with evidence, concluding an argument.

e.g. arguments about understanding change and processes of identity formation and the centrality of 'race' and 'ethnicity'.

FIGURE 10 Skills diagram: constructing social science arguments in Block 1

You can now get started on TMA 01. Good luck.

 Please turn to the *Assignments Booklet* for TMA 01.

COMMENT ON
WORKBOOK ACTIVITY 3.6 _____

Marx and Weber: completed grid

	Marx	Weber
What is the structural basis of class divisions?	Ownership and non-ownership of capital: the means of production	Market position, access to or possession of wealth, qualifications, skills
Is class the main division in society?	Yes – economic divisions are replicated by political and cultural divisions	No – class divisions are cross-cut with status and power
How many classes are there in capitalist societies?	Two – the bourgeoisie or ruling class and the working class	Many – dependent upon the structure of the labour market: types of job, demand for skills, etc.
What relationship exists between classes?	Mutually interdependent, but locked into unequal conflict	Variety of relationships possible: hierarchies of power and deference, inter-class competition or alliances, sometimes conflict
How and under what conditions do class divisions generate identities?	When class consciousness is recognized. Class identity emerges through polarization of economic conditions, collective agency and struggle	Class only one component of identity. Most identities spring from status groups but organized collective action is also important

COMMENT ON
WORKBOOK ACTIVITY 5.1

Themes of Block 1: completed grid

	What uncertainties are explored in this chapter?	Why is diversity important in understanding these uncertainties?	How do we see people in this chapter shaping their identities?	What structures constrain and generate control over our identities?
Chapter 2	Gendered identities becoming uncertain, limits of essentialist categories make for uncertainty.	Individuals possess adverse and sometimes contradictory range of gendered characteristics. The fuzzy nature of gendered identities makes diversity possible.	Children actively identifying with socially constructed categories.	School teachers' expectations, family life, biological and cognitive structures.
Chapter 3	Economic identities like class becoming uncertain as work changes.	Complexity of new patterns of work and consumption lead to uncertainty.	The poor reject identities imposed on them. Classes organize around and can entrench identity.	Inequalities of wealth and power.
Chapter 4	Uncertainties around Britishness and English national identity. Uncertainties about identities.	Social, political and cultural changes, greater ethnic diversity in contemporary UK life.	Collective action by black and Asian people reconstructing their identities. Political and policy changes.	Stereotypes, racisms, social attitudes, policies, lack of understanding of diversity, racialization and ethnicization.

APPENDIX: PROCESS AND COMMAND WORDS IN ESSAY QUESTIONS

Account for	Explain, clarify, give reasons for.
Analyse	Resolve into its component parts. Examine critically or minutely.
Assess	Determine the value of, weigh up (see also Evaluate).
Compare	Look for similarities and differences between, perhaps reach conclusions about which is preferable and justify this clearly.
Contrast	Set in opposition in order to bring out the differences sharply.
Compare and contrast	Find some points of common ground between x and y and show where or how they differ.
Criticize	Make a judgement (backed by a discussion of the evidence or reasoning involved) about the merit of theories or opinions or about the truth of facts.
Define	State the exact meaning of a word or phrase. In some cases it may be necessary or desirable to examine different possible or often used definitions.
Describe	Give a detailed account of ...
Discuss	Explain, then give two sides of the issue and any implications.
Distinguish or differentiate between	Look for differences between ...
Evaluate	Make an appraisal of the worth/validity/effectiveness of something in the light of its truth or usefulness (see also Assess).
Examine the argument that ...	Look in detail at this line of argument.
Explain	Give details about how and why it is ...
How far ...	To what extent ... Usually involves looking at evidence/arguments for and against and weighing them up.
Illustrate	Make clear and explicit, usually requires the use of carefully chosen examples.
Justify	Show adequate grounds for decisions or conclusions, answer the main objections likely to be made about them.

Outline	Give the main features or general principles of a subject, omitting minor details and emphasizing structure and arrangement.
State	Present in a brief, clear way.
Summarize	Give a concise, clear explanation or account of ... presenting the chief factors and omitting minor details and examples (see also Outline).
What arguments can be made for and against the view that ...	Look at both sides of this argument.

Source: Redman, P. *et al.* (1998) *Good Essay Writing: A Social Sciences Guide*, Milton Keynes, The Open University, pp.66–7.

REFERENCES

Durkheim, E. (1915) *The Elementary Forms of the Religious Life: A Study in Religious Sociology* (translated by Swain, J.), London, Allen and Unwin.

Guibernau, M. (1998) *Nationalisms*, Cambridge, Polity.

ACKNOWLEDGEMENTS

Grateful acknowledgement is made to the following sources for permission to reproduce material in this workbook.

Figures

Figure 5: Bright, M., 'Boys performing badly', *The Observer*, 4 January 1998, © *The Observer* 1998; Figure 6: Popperfoto.

Cover

Image copyright © 1996 PhotoDisc, Inc.

STUDY SKILLS INDEX